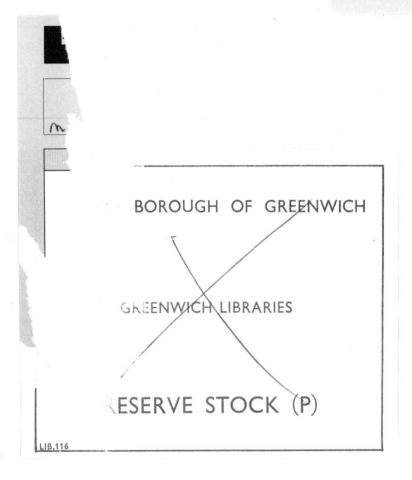

SWIM, BABY, SWIM

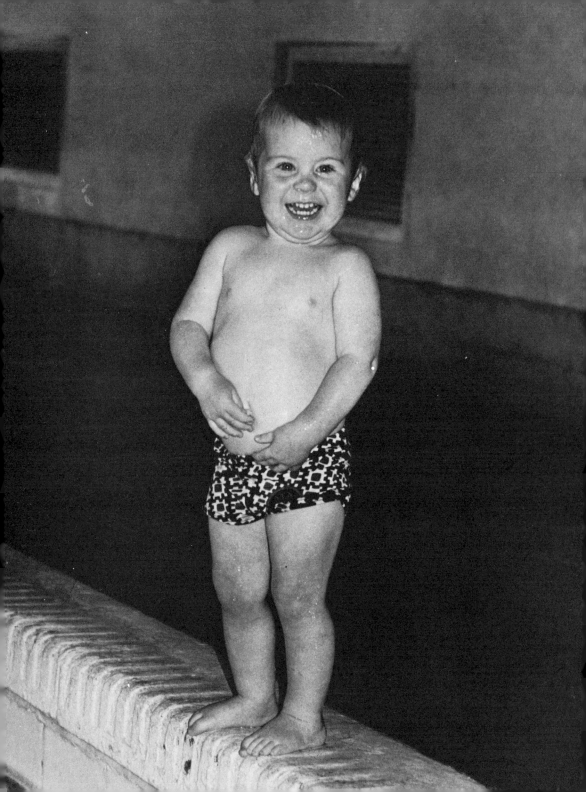

SWIM, BABY, SWIM

ANNE HAWLEY

Published in association with
Savlon BabyCare

PELHAM BOOKS
LONDON

*This book is dedicated to
three very special people
Philip, Adam and Emma*

Frontispiece Eighteen-
month-old Adam
Hawley.

First published in Great Britain by
PELHAM BOOKS LTD
44 Bedford Square
London WC1B 3DP

British Library Cataloguing in Publication Data

Hawley, Anne
    Swim, baby, swim.
    1. Swimming for infants.
    I. Title
    797.2'1'07   GV837.25

    ISBN 0-7207-1542-3

Typeset by Allset Composition, London
Printed in Great Britain by
Hollen Street Press Ltd at Slough
and bound by Hunter & Foulis Ltd, Edinburgh

Savlon is a registered trademark

Contents

Foreword

It is indeed a pleasure to write a Foreword to Anne Hawley's new book *Swim, Baby, Swim*. This is a non-technical book, the aim of which is to introduce parents to baby/parent swimming. She has found, like many others, that babies who learn to develop their swimming abilities, are normally more alert and astute for their age, with a better eating and sleeping pattern. In addition, such exercise improves their cardio-respiratory function and their general health.

Water awareness and acceptability are encouraged from early bathing and in this book all aspects are covered until the child is old enough to have overcome water-shyness and to have learned to respect water. Such supervised exercises as described, by improving the baby's cardio-respiratory function, may help in the reduction of the number of cases of 'cot death' in some instances and in the improvement of some asthmatics.

This book is highly recommended for all parents of young children and those involved in the teaching and organisation of baby/parent water classes.

J. M. CAMERON
G. B. Olympic Swimming Team Doctor
1984

Preface

Why another book on swimming?

Well, I hope that as you turn the pages of this book, you will see that it is geared to a new generation of swimmers – the age group from birth to two years. This is not a technical book for advanced swimming teachers but is designed to show parents (whether or not they have access to parent and baby classes) a unique teaching method that allows young babies to swim unaided from birth.

Just think of the age you were when you learnt to swim; now try to imagine what it must be like being unable to remember learning. As my son Adam, aged three years, said to me on one occasion, 'But Mum, I could always swim, couldn't I?' Over the past ten years that I have been teaching and developing my method of baby swimming, I have endeavoured to correct the impression that children normally learn to swim unaided from around the age of five years.

I hope that most parents and swimming teachers will adopt my proven methods and that it will become more usual to see small babies swimming and less common to witness the frightened toddler and young child at your local pool. Whatever race, creed or colour, any baby can swim using the system described in this book.

I have tried to show through photographs and diagrams how my unique method works, and I am sure that if you are patient enough you will have the joy of seeing your young baby swimming happily by your side. The efforts you put into your baby's swimming sessions will reap tremendous rewards, and I wish all my readers many happy swimming years ahead!

Throughout the text I have used 'he', 'him', etc when referring to babies. This has been done purely for simplicity and I hope that parents of daughters will not feel slighted.

Warning

I would like to stress that readers should adhere strictly to the instructions given in this book.

The training programme includes exercises where the baby is completely submerged underwater *for a few seconds only*, and provided you follow the instructions carefully, no harm will come to baby at all. In fact it is through such exercises that baby can go on to develop his own natural ability to swim. *Never allow your baby to stay face down or submerged in water for longer than is recommended in the text.*

Do not attempt to rush on to the advanced stages of prolonged swims too soon. Make sure that the baby is happy, safe and confident in all the elementary stages before moving on. Keep your exercises short until you see the baby progressing.

Finally, at no time must a baby or toddler be left unattended near water, whether in the home or in a public bathing place.

Follow the guidelines in this book and you and your baby will be safe. Remember, your baby can already swim, he just needs the opportunity to show you how.

Acknowledgments

I wish to acknowledge my indebtedness to the following people: the manager and staff at the Dorking Swimming Centre, Surrey, who helped and co-operated to the full in my unique 'Swim Baby' classes; Atlantis Swimming Club, to whose youngest swimmers who first pioneered my new methods, I wish great success in the future; Tom Shepherd, the principal pools manager of the London Borough of Croydon, for his encouragement in the continuation of these courses in Croydon; the manager and all pool staff at New Addington Pool, Croydon, who have been especially helpful and considerate to all the parents and babies who attend my courses; and to all my colleagues who are swimming teachers, too numerous to mention by name, but who have shown great interest in my methods and are now successfully teaching small babies at their own pools.

I am also grateful to the London Borough of Croydon for allowing me to use their facilities during the preparation of this book.

A special acknowledgment must go to a very patient lady, Sue Parker, who spent many nights correcting my spelling mistakes and putting together my manuscript from endless bits of paper. I really appreciate all her hard work and the professional way in which she presented my manuscript.

Finally, my thanks are due to Savlon BabyCare, who sponsor the Savlon Water Baby Award Scheme and who have generously supported this book.

Picture Credits

The photographs in this book are reproduced by courtesy of the following:

Savlon BabyCare – 81 (bottom), 93
News of the World – frontispiece, 78, 79, 85
Associated Newspapers – 60
Croydon Advertiser – 14, 15, 31
Nigel Scarlett – 27, 30
Ian Smith – 21, 34, 35, 37, 39, 41, 42, 43, 45, 46-47, 49, 52, 53, 57, 72, 74, 75
Tony Hutchings – cover picture, 16, 32, 61, 64, 67, 68, 77, 81 (top), 82

The line illustrations were drawn by Jim Robins.

Introduction

I feel it is necessary to start my book by indicating the number of deaths caused by drowning. I firmly believe that such statistics can be dramatically reduced if we start learning to swim from birth instead of waiting until the average age of seven to nine years, or in many cases until much later in life.

Statistics for 1982 show that over one half of drownings are within 10 feet of the water's edge (55 per cent) and 42 per cent are closer than 6 feet!

It is estimated that, sadly, about one quarter of the drownings that occur in England and Wales are children under the age of fifteen. Personally I feel that no one can be 100 per cent sure of never drowning but, with the right training and natural water ability that we have, we should at least give ourselves a chance of survival if any accident should occur.

The human foetus is developed in a sac of water in which it is contained safely throughout the nine months of pregnancy. Instinctively a baby controls its breathing when placed under water and very young babies haven't learnt to fear water: now is the time to encourage and develop these natural instincts. The more a baby swims the better. A baby's ability to hold his breath while swimming a width of a pool is very common and babies with the right training feel no ill effects whatsoever.

It is obvious from my classes that babies who learn to develop their swimming abilities at an early stage are normally very alert and astute for their age. They also progress much more quickly in their crawling and walking habits. Swimming sessions

for baby are undoubtedly the best exercise he can take before the age of two years. Most babies spend their first six months just eating and sleeping, but 'swim babies' eat, sleep *and* exercise.

A particular advantage is that they sleep very well — which can seem a miracle to parents whose baby appears to stay awake all day and night. On many occasions I have been approached

The author (left) supervising a 'water baby' swimming class.

A group of mothers and babies enjoying their swimming sessions.

on the poolside by a young couple with a new-born baby who have asked me whether swimming will help their baby to sleep. Quite positively I say that it will help those babies who seem overactive or restless. So it can be quite rewarding to struggle along to your local pool with your baby and his luggage and find that, after his swim, you could well be in for a good two or three hours of peace and quiet!

No problems for this
mother and baby —
pool sessions should
be happy and relaxed.

Fathers should be
encouraged to bring
baby to the pool.

1 Bathtime Training

Exercises in the bath at home

It is important to start your baby's swimming exercises at home because you can quite naturally feel insecure handling a newborn child. This fear is often intensified when the baby has been submerged in water and is slippery to hold. So remember to practise in the safe environment of your bathroom until you feel happy about handling a wet infant.

It is also important to discard the baby bath when you start these sessions, so that baby learns to feel safe in a large amount of water from the first stage. There is no point in gaining his confidence in your own bath if you still continue to use the baby bath. The more water you use, the better, and naturally you should keep the temperature of your bath comfortable for both you and the baby.

These exercises do not take long and you should regard them as a daily swimming lesson with your baby in your own home. If baby enjoys his bath, he will be a long way towards enjoying his swimming, but do remember that the bathroom is a small area compared to the large and strange environment of a public swimming pool, so make sure you are well prepared before you go to the main pool for your first session there — see Chapter 3.

Both parents can enjoy bathing their baby. It is an excellent opportunity to introduce him to water in a safe environment and begin to monitor his progress. As soon as you leave hospital after the birth and are familiar with your new baby, the very first exercise should be to have a nice deep warm bath (83° F/ 28°C) and take him with you.

Lie back in the bath and hold and caress your naked baby. Allow him to lie deep in the water, but with his head supported on your chest or shoulder. Just relax and talk to your baby, stroking his head. Don't worry about any water going on to his head or face. Any fear or anxiety that you may have will be communicated to your baby, so you must control such feelings while you are with him in the water.

When you and your partner can accomplish the above, you will be ready to move on to the next stage.

Your first swimming lesson with baby at home

Now you are more familiar with your baby in the bath, it is time to move on to sitting or kneeling in the water, still holding your baby gently and talking softly. Music playing quietly in

1.1 Early exercises in the bath at home. Keep watching baby all the time while you draw him towards you.

another room can be useful in creating the right calm atmosphere.

At this point, having your partner around can give you confidence. Hold baby, at arm's length, with one hand on either side of his rib-cage, and draw him *gently* under water all the way towards you (see illustration 1.1.). He will automatically put his head down, so don't worry. Hesitation at the start of this exercise may cause baby to take a breath at the wrong moment and swallow water, which will not harm him but may make you feel anxious. When you have brought him close, hold him clear of the water and give him a big cuddle – *not* a hearty hug! (See illustrations 1.2 and 1.3 for the right and wrong ways to pick up a baby in the water.)

It is very important that this exercise is performed quietly, gently and above all calmly.

During the following days you should practise this exercise three or four times during each bath session.

1.2 *Never* pick baby up by the head.

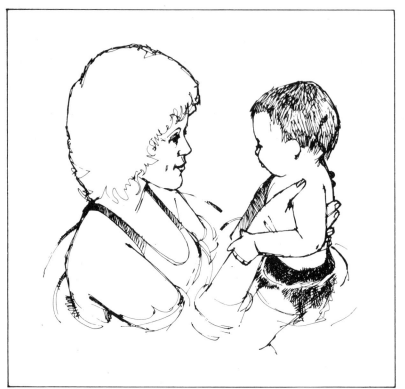

1.3 Correct way to lift baby out of the water.

Observations

During these sessions look out for the following and make a record of them (use your chart on page 89):

1. Are baby's eyes open or closed?
2. Is his mouth open?
3. Are there any air bubbles from his nose or mouth?
4 Does baby cry after his submersion and if so how long does it take for him to settle down? Please do not worry if he does cry because, after all, he has by now been out of his original water environment for several days and may take a little while to get used to it again. However, you may have a baby who takes to his bath like a duck to water!

1.4 OPPOSITE Mothers at a local baby class demonstrating the correct way of picking baby up out of the water.

Shivering

Very small babies get cold rapidly and five minutes is often
long enough in the bath at first. If baby still shivers, keep a vest
on him all the time and you may find when you first visit a
pool that he will need to wear a short-sleeved T-shirt or vest as
well as pants but this will not impair his swimming.

2 Hints for Safety and Comfort

Vaccinations

It is always wise to avoid taking your new-born baby to any public place until he has received some sort of immunization. Your doctor will advise you on what is necessary. In the case of a small baby going into a public swimming pool for the first time, I always ask parents if their baby has had his first dose of vaccine and is well. He should not go if he is suffering from a sniffly cold or bad chest, and certainly not if he has any ear trouble or eye infection.

Some clinics do immunize at three months, others not until baby is six months old. You can, of course, ask your doctor if you want to take your baby to a public pool and he may consent to immunization at three months. Certainly the first three months of swimming can be safely undertaken at home in your bath.

However, public swimming pools now have excellent facilities for maintaining clean and healthy conditions. Today's modern chemical plant will keep the pool water safe for you and your baby to use, and the local health authority makes random checks on all its public pools to ensure that the water is up to the required health standards.

Feeding and hygiene

To avoid 'accidents', your baby must be fed *two hours* before his swim in a public pool if he is to take a full feed. This allows time for digestion and any soiling before you get to the pool. I advise only a small feed (enough to satisfy) and another feed after swimming when baby is very tired and hungry. He will then sleep quietly for the next few hours, giving mum and dad a well-earned rest!

If your baby is on solids, don't be afraid to take some hot water in a flask to the pool and heat his food and feed as usual.

It is important to keep your experience of baby swimming a happy one. It is far better to be strict about toilet routine, even with a tiny infant, than to become unpopular at a public pool because baby has had an 'accident'. After all, it is rather an unpleasant experience for all concerned and one that can be avoided if the appropriate precautions are taken. So choose the time of your pool visit carefully and plan your feeding routine with the swimming session in mind.

Special care of the ears

After your baby's swimming sessions, pay special attention to the drying of the ears. Always wipe his ears dry, but never poke inside. Turn baby gently on to one side, wait for the water to drain away, dry this ear and repeat for the other side. It is essential to clear any water from the auditory canal (leading to the eardrum), because if left unattended it could cause severe pain. Remember to protect baby's ears after a swim with a woolly hat or hood, particularly on a cold day. If your baby has any trouble with his ears, particularly a prolonged ear infection, you must check with your doctor before the next swim.

What does baby wear?

Because your baby is used to playing in the bath without clothes on he would immediately feel strange if, to visit a public pool, you changed your relaxed routine by making him wear a nappy-towel or disposable which would very quickly become soggy and uncomfortable. I advise all parents to buy some cheap towelling pants or even to use a pair of bikini briefs on baby.

2.1 'Come on, mum, teach me to swim!' says Adam Hawley, aged six months.

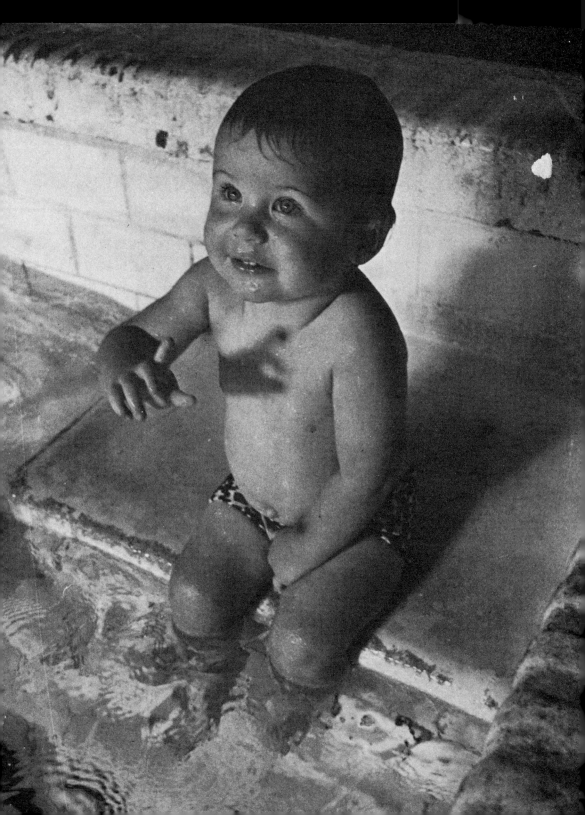

These are ideal and he can wear them until he is old enough to have his first swimsuit.

What do I wear?

You may feel that this is an odd question, but my advice is to wear something bright to help baby 'home in' under the water. Reds, greens and turquoises are all good colours to wear in the swimming pool. The colours to avoid are black, white and browns as these fail to impress young swimmers. Mum's costume can be patterned or plain, one-piece or two-piece. She should make sure that the top half of the costume is well secured with a fastener or a good knot as baby will cling on to this part and she could suddenly be left topless with baby chewing the other half! So beware, I have warned you!

Dad too can wear bright-coloured trunks but the most important thing for both parents to remember is not to change costume at all because this has been known to confuse young babies who then start swimming away (looking for the well-known costume colours) and naturally this can upset them.

Warning: jewellery

Many young babies today wear jewellery of some kind. Neck chains are particularly hazardous, and if caught in the folds of a young baby's neck could result in an accident. Therefore remove all jewellery during every swim, including at home in the bath.

As for adult jewellery, rings on fingers can catch and scratch baby, so it is advisable to turn your rings round if possible so that the flat, unadorned part is on the outside of the finger. Better still, take off all rings.

Many swimming pools have 'treasure troves' of unclaimed jewellery — make sure it's not yours. It's better to be safe than sorry.

Open-water swims

It is very important to remember that all the exercises described

2.2 Your baby can enjoy the water just like seven-month-old Oliver, pictured here with the author.

in this book are intended for use only in a controlled environment, i.e. a public swimming pool. The water is clear, baby can
be observed at all times and obviously there are no unseen
dangers such as rocks or strong currents which can be encoun-
tered in open water such as the sea.

I *do not* advise that any of the exercises described are carried
out in open water because of these hazards. Play safe and take
your baby to a local swimming pool. Do not be tempted to swim
your baby in *any* open water.

3 Your First Visit to a Public Pool

Preparation

Before your baby's first visit to a public swimming pool, go along there to familiarize yourself with the following:

1. Opening times, particularly during school terms. Ask when the pool is quiet and not too crowded.

2. The temperature of the small pool, or the main one if there is no teaching pool.

3. Are the changing rooms warm? Where can you leave the pram or buggy?

4. Can you bring baby's towel on to the poolside?

5. How large are the lockers? You may need two lockers, one for baby's things and one for your own.

6. Are there are safe areas, i.e. play-pen, where you can leave baby while you dress/undress?

Some pools are better equipped than others, so look around and go to one that suits your needs even though it may mean travelling a little further.

Who can be your partner?

It is a good idea — though not absolutely essential — to have a partner with you in the pool to help with your exercises. Ideally the partners should be mum and dad, although I know of mums and their sisters who have worked well together, and mums and grandmas; and the *au pair* or nanny, who can be super with

their charges, should not be forgotten. Obviously your partner
has to be someone whom baby recognizes and is familiar with.

Non-swimming parents?

Parents who are non-swimmers can still successfully follow the
advice outlined in this book, but they must be careful to stay
only in a shallow pool and where they themselves feel happy.
Of course, if possible, a non-swimming parent should at least
learn to float and to regain a standing position with the feet on
the bottom of the pool, in the event of slipping and going under
water while holding baby.

3.1 A group lesson
in progress at Dorking
Swimming Centre.

Remember that any tension you may have while you are in the pool will be passed to your baby. Even with the best will in the world, you may transmit your fear of the water to him. My best advice to you therefore is to learn to swim first if you can.

3.2 A group of young mothers and their babies taking part in a swimming session supervised by the author, at New Addington Pool, Croydon.

Overcoming water-shyness in older children

Your child may be anxious about visiting a public swimming pool because he doesn't like getting his face wet. The following are two ways in which he can become used to this at home beforehand.

HAIR WASHING

Many children hate having their hair washed. I blame you, mum and dad! Why? Well, it is quite easy to obtain shampoos that are soapless, gentle and do not sting the eyes.

There is no reason why a child shouldn't get his face wet during hair washing — after all, it is the ideal time. If you have an older child for whom hair washing is still a problem, try to get him to wash his own hair and to put his head forwards over the basin, not backwards.

SHOWERS

A shower is a great way for a child who is nervous of putting his face in the water to overcome this anxiety. Make shower time fun time, and gradually, if you shower with your child, he will lose his fear.

3.3 Baby's swimming lessons can be enjoyed by all the family, and having your partner around can be reassuring.

4 Exercises: Three to Six Months

Always bear in mind that it takes time and practice to establish the following exercises. They cannot all be undertaken at once in one swimming session but should be spread over a period of ten to twelve weeks, depending on how old your baby is when you first go to a public pool.

Bouncing baby

Take your baby into the warm pool and start by bouncing him gently up and down and from side to side. Talk to him all the time and even sing if you want to. Above all, be relaxed — that goes for your partner too!

You are now ready for the next stage of the bouncing exercise. This time, bounce as usual and then completely submerge your baby, keeping hold of him all the time and very slowly bringing him to the surface (see illustrations 4.1 and 4.2).

OBSERVATIONS
1. Are baby's eyes open?
2. Did he kick?
3. Is his mouth open?
4. Are there bubbles?
5. Are the bubbles from the nose or mouth?
6. Did he cry?
7. If he cried, did he settle soon afterwards?

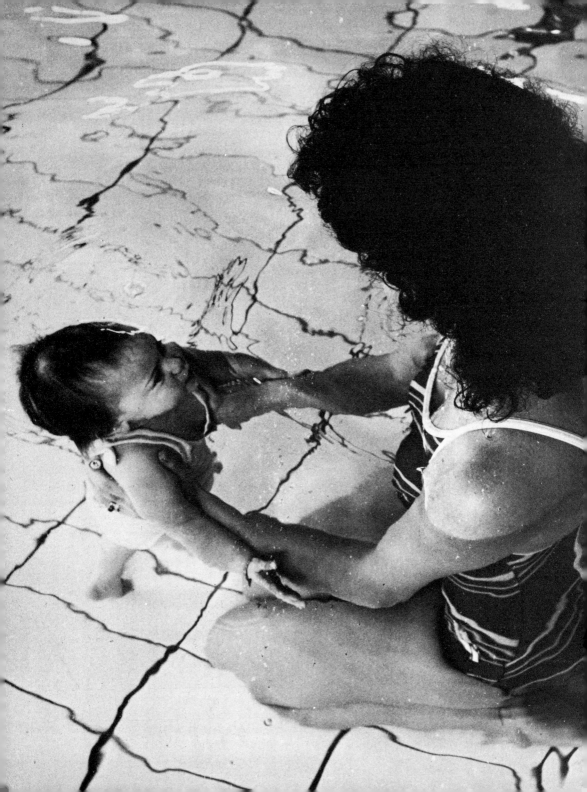

4.1 OPPOSITE Sarah King, aged one year, fully submerged in shallow water. Her eyes are open and she is smiling at the author.

4.2 Correct way to bring baby to the surface in the bouncing exercise.

Do this exercise three or four times on your first visit to the pool and keep a record of your baby's reactions (see chart, page 89).

CASE EXAMPLES

1. *The wriggler* Some babies wriggle quite considerably when you first submerge them in water, but this only happens to those who have temporarily lost their natural ability for movement under water. In such a case, simply persevere with your practice sessions in the bath at home before returning to the pool, and baby will progress very rapidly. However, you may find that a few more 'dips' on this first pool visit, followed by lots of cuddles and encouragement (*not* a full hearty hug), will nearly always do the trick and baby will respond. If this happens, you can progress to the next stage.

2. *Cry baby* This, quite honestly, is normally the fault of the mums. Naturally you are apprehensive during your first few visits to the pool, but even so you must try to appear confident to your baby. Sometimes he may even cry before you begin the exercises.

Remember: as described earlier, submerge and raise your baby from the water slowly, not quickly or harshly, which can frighten him — it is similar to dropping him into thin air and then grabbing him at the last minute. Carry out all movements slowly and confidently, and follow them with a gentle kiss and cuddle.

Another important point is: don't stand still after this exercise waiting for a reaction from your baby. Simply move around the pool and treat everything as normal and he will react in the same way.

3. *Smiling baby* Well done, mum! You've obviously done everything right and you can happily move on to the next stage.

First swim

Baby's first swim will cover about 2 metres/6½ feet. There are two parts to this exercise: *floating* face down, which is very important; and *submersion and release*, to allow baby to swim to the surface unaided.

FLOATING

Lie baby flat on his front and allow his face to go into the water, gently let go of him (see illustrations 4.3 and 4.4), count to three, and slowly lift him up. Repeat.

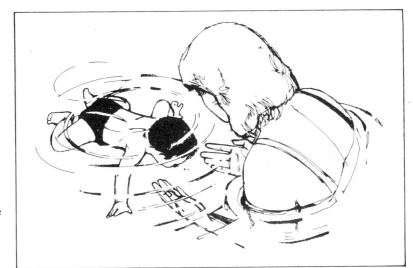

4.3 Letting baby go for the first time.

4.4 BELOW When letting baby go for the first time, keep him close to you, but don't be afraid to let go.

SUBMERSION AND RELEASE
Bounce baby up and down as described under 'Bouncing baby'
on page 33, and on the down movement allow him to go
right under, so that there is at least 50 centimetres/18 inches of
water above his head. At first don't let go of him while you
slowly bring him to the surface. As your confidence increases
allow him to surface gently unaided by releasing him while he
is under water.

Repeat these exercises until your baby is quite happy doing
them, but take care not to tire him.

Some babies surface very quickly, others very slowly and
some not at all — in fact, they sink to the bottom or simply roll
over and over. I will take each one of these examples step by
step.

Surfacing quickly
At the recommended water depth, which is at the most 50–60
centimetres/18 inches–2 feet, no harm will come to baby if he
rises very quickly, but be ready to catch him as soon as he
surfaces and do not allow him to bob up and down two or three
times before you pick him up. You can teach baby to surface
slowly by guiding him yourself and by not releasing him until
you feel him slowing down.

Surfacing slowly
Again, at the depth I advise this exercise to be carried out,
there is no cause for alarm if baby surfaces slowly, but you can,
if you wish, give him a gentle push upwards with your foot or
hand. Do this a few times and really praise your baby as he
surfaces.

Sinking and rolling
It can be quite alarming to watch your baby sinking and rolling
to the bottom of the pool when you expect him to rise. The
reasons for his doing so are normally that he was submerged
suddenly without being able to fill his lungs with air; or you
pushed him down too deep on his first exercise of surfacing by

4.5 Correct way of
handling baby in the
water.

himself; or (very rarely) he has very little bouyancy at this stage, but it can be developed so don't let it worry you.

If you feel that he failed to rise for either of the first two reasons, do try again. If baby still sinks gently place your foot underneath him and push upwards (see illustration 4.6). Repeat this exercise as soon as you see him going the wrong way. Remember to let him rest between these exercises and don't tire him out. He will soon learn to surface correctly.

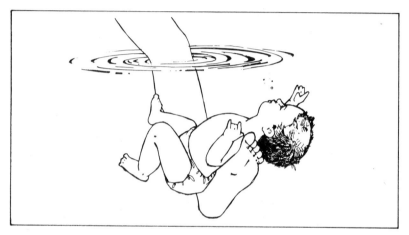

4.6 How to recover a sinking baby in shallow water.

Next try going under water with baby yourself and guiding him upwards. Do this exercise gently and open your eyes so that you can see him. Remember also to go under slowly with him (cuddling) and surface quietly.

If your baby has very little buoyancy and seems to sink like a stone, you will need to guide him constantly. Now is the time when you are actually teaching him. He may feel very frightened at first because he has the sensation of falling when he is under water. Take care, guide him and don't let him get into the sinking stage; keep practising, always in the shallow pool, until eventually baby grows and matures to his full buoyancy potential. He will swim just like the other babies, but you need to take care to practise with him as often as you can in water of 60 centimetres/2 feet in depth.

Short swim

This is ideal if you are working with a partner. Stand about 1 metre/3 feet apart, face to face. When you are ready, place baby face down and push him gently forward towards your partner. Let him go so that you can see him swimming to your partner (see illustration 4.7). Then change over and let your partner have a go. When you pick baby up, do it gently and re-member to hold him under the arms, not by the head or neck.

If you do not have a partner, hold baby at arm's length facing towards you, put him face down in the water, gently place the palms of both your hands around the back of his head and let him gently swim towards you (see illustration 4.8). Let go of baby before you pick him up so that you can take hold of him under the arms and not by the head.

Repeat the above exercises until you feel happy with your baby's progress, remembering not to tire him out. Some babies will swim like tadpoles, their feet kicking away quite naturally, and they aim straight for the 'receiving' adult; others, however, will roll or flip over on to their backs. (see 'Kicking' on page 50.)

4.7 Group lesson in shallow water, showing use of partners (baby swapping!).

Swimming on the back: stage 1

Some babies love turning over and swimming on their backs.
They enjoy seeing their environment clearly around them and
seem happy to support themselves in this position. Unfortunately,
very young babies cannot support themselves on their backs
successfully for long periods of time (more than about twenty-
five seconds) as their neck muscles are too weak and therefore
their heads flop backwards, causing the head and face to be
covered by water. They then usually take in water through the
nose and down the back of the throat — an unpleasant sensation,
to say the least, which can be quite upsetting for them. Certainly
there are exercises which should be practised on the back, but
all with parental support until you feel that baby is strong
enough to swim unaided. (See 'Swimming on the back: stage 2'
on page 44.)

4.8 The correct way
to hold baby during
early swims; gently
behind the back of
the head.

Floating

This is a very good exercise for relaxing baby. Stand to one side of him (never behind the head) and gently support him with one hand outstretched between his shoulder blades (see illustration 4.9). Allow the rest of his body to relax and float. Talk and whisper to him all the time so that he feels completely relaxed. .

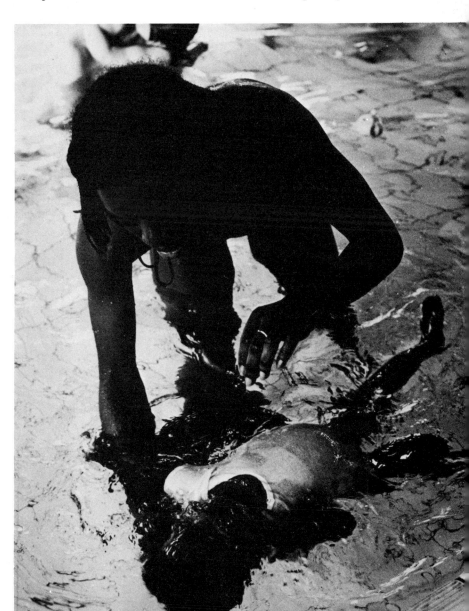

4.9 Baby floating on her back with support.

You will soon sense that you can gradually remove a little support by taking one finger at a time away from his back until only one is left. The water level is usually all around baby's face but not over it. Then, as you feel him supporting himself, you can take your hand away altogether and he will float for about 10 to 15 seconds unaided. When baby feels himself sinking, he will begin to kick, which will be the start of moving on his back without help.

Floating face down can also be achieved successfully by allowing baby to lie in the water without any support for about five seconds. Let go of him gently, count to five and lift him up. Remember to praise him, and when you let him go to float, do this smoothly and gently with no sudden 'drop' movement.

Don't forget to watch baby as he floats around and observe what he is doing.

Swimming on the back: stage 2

Start the exercise by getting your baby to float unaided on his back. Once you and your baby have mastered this for about 10 to 15 seconds, you can move on to the next stage. A young baby's neck muscles are still fairly weak, but once he has learned to lie happily on his back he will really enjoy these sessions. Some babies relax so much that they fall asleep!

When baby is floating on his back, stay close and hold your hands above him, make a clicking noise with your fingers to catch his attention, and see how long he will hold this position. If clicking doesn't keep his attention for long enough, try holding a toy that he recognizes or even sing to him — some mums have, in my experience, found that their babies respond really well to this approach.

Swimming backwards

Once your baby is floating confidently and well, tickle his toes until he moves slightly. Try to avoid his kicking too hard as this usually causes him to push his head backwards so that he goes under water. All you want is a gentle kick with just a little

4.10 Baby floating on his back unaided.

water covering his face now and then — and see how far your baby will go!

Remember: try short swims to start with and don't forget to rest baby as you don't want him to get a stiff neck from lying on his back for too long.

Swimming exercise around your waist

Follow illustrations 4.11, 4.12 and 4.13 for guidance.
1. Place your left hand behind the back of baby's head and guide him close to your waist.
2. Change hands behind your back. Do not turn round.

4.11—13 Baby swimming around the waist: lead off with the left hand...

4.12... change hands behind your back...

4.13 . . . and follow round with the right hand, bringing baby safely back in front of you.

3. Follow round with the right hand, bringing baby safely back in front of you.

By using this method you will be swimming baby round in a circle, using your waistline as a guide. Remember to keep him tucked in closely so that he doesn't drift too far out.

Winding baby

It is very common to see small babies with bloated tummies after their first few swims. Obviously, to allow your baby to be comfortable in the water you must spend a little time winding him until you hear that loud burp! It is not fair on him to continue the swimming exercises while his tummy is hard and bloated. If you did continue, baby could develop tummy-ache and would soon let you know by crying during his swim session.

Older babies, however, quickly become experts at winding themselves. By the age of ten months, many a 'swim baby' may, after coming to the surface, produce a really loud burp and then carry on swimming as if it were the most normal thing to do. So if your baby does start to make these unsocial noises, please ignore him and carry on!

Hiccups

This is another sound that can suddenly occur after a few swims. The best course of action is to stop swimming, move to the side of the pool and try to hold baby as straight as you can. If hiccups still persist, allow him a small drink of water. If he always breaks out in hiccups, keep a plastic bottle ready to use as soon as he starts. Remember: do not continue the swimming session until the hiccups have ceased.

Rolling over

This is caused by baby turning towards the light and not being sure of where to go. The first remedy is to guide him by holding him gently with the palm of your hand at the back of his head. This support stops him from rolling. Young babies, of course, need particular support because their neck muscles are so weak.

Practise holding baby's head this way when you first start his swimming sessions, and when you sense that he no longer turns his head, you can let him go forward with no help at all.

4.14 Make time for a chat in between exercises.

Kicking

As previously mentioned, some babies kick instinctively from the first experience of swimming while others do not. If your baby doesn't kick, you must show him what you expect him to do.

First, once you have released him to your partner, try tickling the soles of his feet. This normally has the immediate effect of making him kick. Once he does this, pick him up, praise him and repeat the exercise each time he swims until you find you don't need to do it any more. If this method fails, try tickling baby's tummy after you have released him and as he makes his way to your partner. Remember to praise him, and repeat the exercise as in the first method. Another ploy you can try is to tickle the back of his neck, again praising his success.

In fact, it is always a good idea to pick up and praise baby when he has made any sort of voluntary movement, but don't get into the habit of picking him up when he is lying still. Babies are quick to learn that if they are still you will pick them up anyway and then they won't bother to kick! So you must make baby associate being picked up with a movement of some kind.

Deep swimming exercises

Again, these exercises are practised only in 60 centimetres to 1 metre/2–3 feet of water – the teaching pool is ideal. The idea is to encourage your baby's kicking and general swimming rhythm.

If you are on your own, kneel on one leg, keeping your other foot firmly on the bottom of the pool. Now gently push baby under water and through the arch made by your leg so that he surfaces just in front of you. Watch him closely and you will see him swimming unaided up to the surface. Be careful not to push him too hard or too near the bottom of the pool because you don't want him to scratch his nose! Illustrations 4.15, 4.16 and 4.17 show how it's done.

If you have a partner you can do this exercise in the shallow end of the main pool. Stand facing your partner at a distance of about 1 metre/3 feet. Now submerge your baby in the water, keeping one hand on the back of his head, and push him gently beneath the surface towards your partner. Remember to release your hand as you get closer to your partner and allow your partner to 'catch' baby. The aim of this exercise is to teach your baby to swim from the bottom of the pool upwards to the surface. Keep observing him all the time and allow him to rest before you repeat the procedure.

Baby will enjoy this exercise and you must, as usual, be prepared to praise him when he succeeds. Look out for any kicking action and note whether he uses his arms to pull himself to the surface as well as a strong kick. Don't forget: if you see baby rolling, stop him and start again. You don't want him to

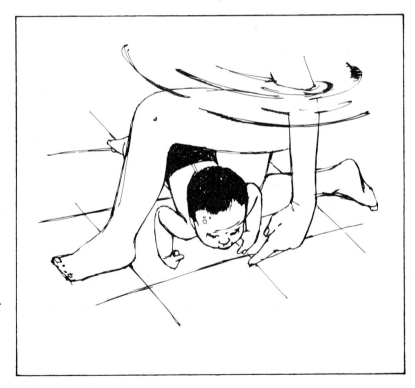

4.15 Swimming under the leg. Gently guide baby under the leg and watch him swim unaided to the surface.

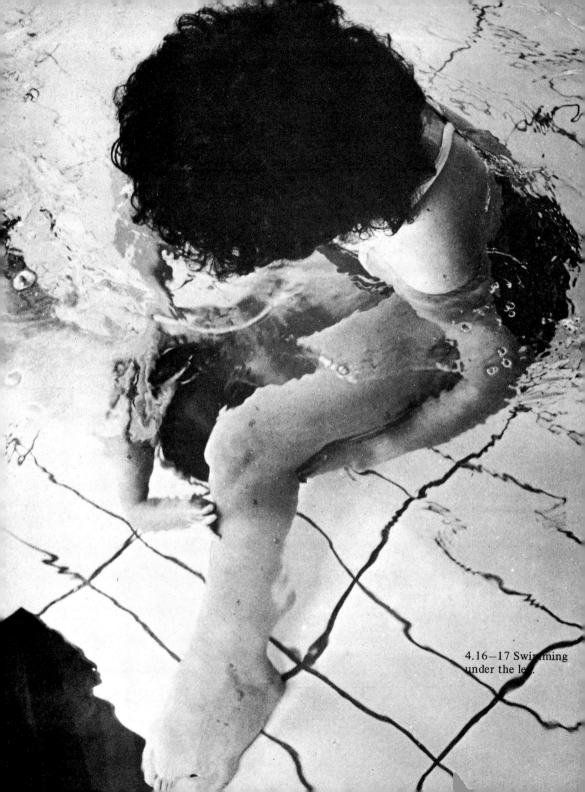

4.16—17 Swimming
under the le..

surface upside down as water will get into his nose and throat
and cause him discomfort and alarm.

4.18 *Never* surface
baby upside down.

Using a toy as a teaching aid

Any sort of bright, clean and safe toy may be used at a public
pool, but always check with pool staff that they have no
objection. Obviously, if you brought in a giant beach ball,
they might have reason to disapprove, but a small, clean toy
that baby is happy with should pose no problem. Choose a toy
in a bright colour — fluorescent orange or green are ideal as they
can be seen easily under water. You should, of course, make
sure that it floats, as you don't want to lose it or tread on it,
and that it has no metal sections which would soon go rusty. It
is also worth mentioning that squeaky toys have been known to
lose their squeak once immersed in water!

Here's how you can use the toy to help your baby learn to
swim. Hold the toy for baby to recognize first. Then, once he is
familiar with it take it away and, when he is completely sub-

merged, hold the toy underwater about 30 centimetres/1 foot in front of him, catch his attention and watch him swim for it. This exercise is quite fascinating, as once baby recognizes the toy and is swimming unaided he will also learn to change direction and swim after it unaided when you change its position.

Make sure he surfaces with the toy, even if on the first few attempts you have to help him to grab it.

Conclusion

Practise these exercises over a period of six weeks, at least twice a week, and gradually your confidence will increase as your baby makes good progress. As you become more proficient with the exercises, you can allow your young baby to swim a distance of about 15 feet/5 metres, but always remember to observe him carefully and not to submerge him so often in one session that he becomes exhausted. Certainly try not to have a swim session without at least one longer swim.

Exercises to practise

1. Submersion and release – allowing baby to swim to the surface unaided.
2. Deep swimming exercises.
3. Floating – front and back position.
4. Swimming unaided – 2–5 metres/2–5½ yards.
5. Correcting faults, i.e. rolling, no kicking, etc.
6. Gaining confidence yourself – letting go of baby, etc.
7. Jumping in (elementary stages) – see page 73.

5 Exercises: Six to Nine Months

As explained earlier, it is always best to start your baby swimming as soon as possible, and by six to nine months he has become very used to his usual bath routine and is aware of his general environment. However, you need to introduce your baby to getting his face wet and to control his breathing when under water. The only way to do this is to submerge him gently.

Exercises at home

Get in the bath with your baby and play water games. Use a plastic beaker and pour water over his head. Blow bubbles hard and pour water over your head. Try to make him copy you and show him how much fun it is. You must be sure that he likes to get his head and face wet before you begin to submerge baby completely, otherwise he will start with quite a shock and it may take a while to settle him. So do spend time at home getting him used to it before you make your first visit to a public pool.

First visit to a public pool

Try to get baby used to the atmosphere of the pool area. Spend a few minutes cuddling, reassuring and talking to him. Now follow the exercises described in Chapter 4, step by step.
1. Submersion – check observations using your chart.
2. Floating.

3. Submersion and release.
4. Short swims.
5. Swimming on the back.

5.1 Whilst in the water, spend time cuddling, reassuring and talking to your baby.

Remember to practise each stage carefully until you and your baby are happy to go on to further exercises. It takes time to complete each exercise so don't hurry your baby. Enter your observations clearly on your chart so that you can judge his progress, session by session, and keep to the short swims until he has properly completed *all* the earlier exercises.

The exercises for a six- to nine-month-old do not differ in any way from those for a younger baby, but because your child is a little older, he is obviously more aware and you will need to give him plenty of encouragement and be patient if he is worried when you first start. Of course, many babies of this age group don't mind being immersed in water at all. They are complete masters of all the exercises within a few weeks.

6 Exercises: Nine Months to One Year

Babies who start swimming lessons at this age may need a special introduction to the water.

Nervous babies

There are babies who are very timid and very 'clingy' to their mothers. They dislike going under water, and when placed beneath the surface they normally shut their eyes tight. After coming up again, they cry and some even take a few seconds to catch their breath. If your baby is one of these, don't despair! He simply needs time to adjust to a water environment again.

Submersion

Allowing baby to cuddle you, slowly place your hand behind the back of his head (to stop him pushing his head back when under water and taking water in). Now, *keeping your eyes open*, take him slowly under water with you. Remember to *surface slowly* and give baby time to catch his breath when he surfaces. Practice is the key word here. With time he will improve and, because you are exercising together, he will gain his confidence through you.

Water games

1. Blow loud bubbles — see if baby will copy you.

6.1–6.2 OPPOSITE
Swim along with mum.

2. Give baby a piggy-back ride through the water. Move to the deeper part of the pool (to a depth of approximately 1 metre/3 feet) and see if you can put baby on to your back. Then swim gently across the pool yourself. Some babies will automatically hold on to Mum's hair, neck chain, straps or costume, but others will not. Don't worry if yours is a 'non-holder'; just get your partner to hold him in place for the present. If you don't have a partner, hold baby on your side and swim slowly side-stroke. This may take some practice, but you'll soon get the idea.

3. Play ball games (a small, soft ball is ideal).

4. Allow baby to play with his own toys in the water.

6.3 BELOW Piggy-
back rides are
especially helpful for
establishing confi-
dence in older babies.

Eventually, as his confidence increases, you can encourage him to spend more time in shallow water without clinging to you. You will find that he makes rapid progress where confidence is concerned as soon as he learns to submerge his face in water

without coughing or swallowing. But it does take a little patience on your part and practice.

Once this stage is mastered, follow the exercises for babies aged three to six months and progress accordingly, using your chart. Corrections of faults are exactly the same for babies of all ages, as are the observations.

Happy babies

Some babies, whatever their age, will take to the water like fish. If your baby is one of these, don't use any aids: simply follow the exercises outlined in this book. However, take particular care in deeper water, because if he is quite fearless he may jeopardize his safety. Make sure your baby thoroughly completes all stages of the swimming exercises and do not be tempted to miss parts out because he seems to be doing so well. Follow my instructions carefully and you will have a fabulous 'water baby' on your hands!

7 Exercises: One to Two Years

Take care with a toddler and do not allow a child who has never put his face under water to try this on his first visit to a public pool, because you may never get him back into the water again without a fight and many tears. Let him enjoy his first visit: allow him to play with his toys; take him around the pool; let him take in the atmosphere.

Exercises without aids

1. Holding hands, walking in shallow water.
2. Holding hands, walking and blowing bubbles.
3. Splashing you and himself.
4. Hair washing.

Exercises with aids

By all means, use armbands to start baby off in the water, but don't fall into the trap of always allowing him to wear them — see Chapter 10 for general advice on their use. It is a good idea to get your baby used to armbands at home in the bath, then he will not find it unusual to put them on in the public pool. Introduce water play when the armbands are not being worn and swimming strokes when they are being worn. When you first put them on baby, take him for a piggy-back ride and, when he seems happy, try to complete the following exercises.

7.1 Two toddlers on their first visit to a pool. Sensibly their mothers have allowed them to bring a few suitable toys from home.

FLOATING ON THE TUMMY

Gently help baby to float and stretch with his feet off the bottom of the pool. Don't expect the feet to come off the bottom too high to start with: just a little at a time is ideal. Get baby to stretch his arms as well as his legs so that he is 'star-shaped'.

FLOATING ON THE TUMMY AND REGAINING THE FEET

This is a very important exercise to a small child because he needs to know that, once his feet are off the bottom, he will be able to put them down again. Teach your child, while holding your hands or the poolside, to raise one leg and then put it down. Practise this with each leg in turn. Now encourage him to put both feet up and down again at the same time.

Once a child can float without your help and using only armbands, you can go on to the next stage.

KICKING

Holding a rail or the poolside, baby should kick up and down. Then, holding your child's hands while you walk backwards, let him splash and kick as much as possible. It is very important that he learns to kick as this propels him through the water, so don't worry about how much he splashes to start with.

Position of kicking

Ideally the legs should be stretched, with only a slight bend in the knees. The toes should be pointed and the feet stretched. Don't worry about too much detail of stroke technique in a child as young as this, but later on it does benefit the child if you can encourage him to stretch when kicking.

Bicycle kicking

This is common in toddlers and from the poolside it looks like they are riding a bicycle. As a child relaxes and lies flat on the water, the more acceptable style of kicking will develop. Practice will make perfect.

ARM MOVEMENTS

I always teach my toddlers to 'run with their hands'. This automatically produces the first stage of the front crawl, and the arms will then match the leg kick. Walk in front of baby, showing him how it's done, and get him to mimic you. It's great fun, and he will soon copy you.

Face in the water

My aim with all toddlers is to get them swimming, and no one can swim without ever getting their face wet! If a child should fall into deep water, the first thing to happen will be that he goes under. It's up to you to teach your child to go under and surface without swallowing any water.

EXERCISES AT HOME IN THE BATH
Teach baby to close his mouth and put his face in the water in your bath at home. *Do not teach baby to hold his nose!* Show him first yourself how it's done – if you are not very good, have a quiet practice alone in the bathroom first. Tell baby to copy you: he must take a deep breath and hold it, and not breathe in through his nose while under water. When he sees you do it, he will try himself.

As soon as baby can hold his breath for short periods, you can progress to the next stage.

Swimming without aids

Enter the main pool at the shallow end – approximately 1 metre/3 feet deep. Take only a few steps from the edge and gently push baby, face in the water, towards the side. Allow him to grasp the poolside himself. He may not be able to hold the side at first, but continue this exercise until he understands what he is supposed to do. Gradually, as he doesn't mind going under water, you can encourage him a little further away from the side.

KICKING – 'RUN, BABY, RUN'
Now is the time to encourage the independent kicking. Shout to

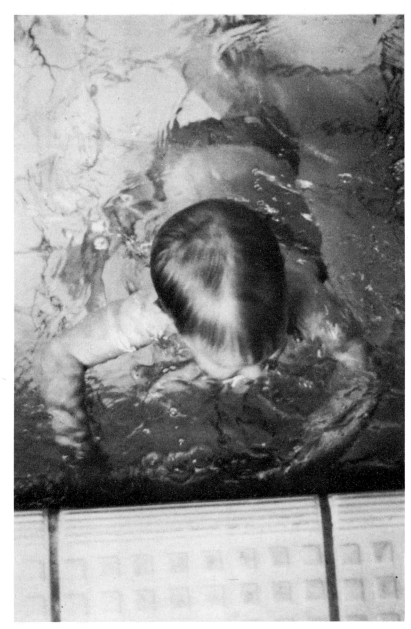

7.2 Swimming to the poolside unaided and reaching for the handrail.

7.3 This young
swimmer has learned
to regain a standing
position in shallow
water.

baby, as you push him, to 'run' with his legs as fast as he can.
This will improve his leg kick enormously.

ARM PULL

Don't worry too much at this stage about the arms. If baby
uses them, all well and good, but as all his power is from his legs
it really doesn't matter as long as he reaches the side. Just make
sure that he has his arms stretched out in front ready to grasp it.
You may prefer your baby to swim to your partner instead of
the poolside.

FLOATING

This is a necessary exercise and should be carried out as described
on page 43.

Jumping in

This is an exercise that children of this age group really enjoy
once they have overcome the problem of going under water.
When they have, follow the exercises step by step described in
Chapter 9. Don't miss anything out and practise until both you
and baby are happy. Use your charts to record your baby's
progress week by week.

7.4 With confidence,
babies are happy to
swim some distance
from mum or dad, to
the poolside.

8 Advanced Routines

Three to six months

Now that your baby is capable of swimming the first few metres unaided, do not try to cover too great a distance too soon. Aim for your baby at six months to be able to swim around 8 metres/9 yards unaided, but no more. Allow him to cover 2–5 metres/2–5½ yards at a time, bring his head up to breathe and then put it straight back down to allow him to continue his swimming. Don't stop too long or baby will lose his momentum through the water.

Now let's take this exercise stage by stage. Start your swim as normal — with baby's face in the water, walk backwards in front of him with your hands cupped behind the back of his head. Take a few paces, then let go of baby and pick him up under his arms, holding his head clear of the water for a count of two, and then put him straight back under and continue as before. Cover in all about 8 metres/9 yards, stopping two or three times.

As your baby gets used to this exercise, you will have to stop only once or twice at the most. Remember: do not perform this exercise until both you and your baby are confident and well-practised in the earlier ones. Some babies kick really fast during these sessions, so be prepared to move backwards quickly and make sure no one is in your way!

Continue practising the short swims and the deep swims (see pages 41 and 50) and always introduce at least one long swim at each swimming session. Eventually you can increase the number of long swims to three or four, as and when baby is ready. It is important that he should enjoy himself, and if he shows any signs of distress on his long swims it is better to continue the short swims just a little longer.

Six to nine months

The routines are the same as for the three-to-six-months group, but as baby is a little older he will be able to adapt to the longer swim a little quicker.

Again, don't rush him. Take your time. Remember you are aiming for approximately 10-metre/11-yard swims.

Because your baby is older, why not try him in the shallow end of the main pool? We don't want him to associate his swimming with a shallow pool, for as time passes you may find he won't like the main pool. So take him into the main pool for at least ten minutes every time you visit — no longer, as the temperature is often lower than that of the small pool.

When in the deeper water of the main pool, try the submersion and floating exercises, deep-water exercises and, of course, jumping in. Above all, have fun and allow baby to swim along with you.

Nine months and over

Spend more time in the main pool. Let your baby show off his talents! He may enjoy jumping in as the best exercise, or he may prefer just swimming under water. Encourage his confidence, but don't allow him to tire himself out too quickly. Continue the following exercises:
1. Longer swims — 5 metres/5½ yards plus.
2. Deep swimming.
3. Submersion under water and swimming to the surface unaided.
4. Playing with toys under water.

9 Jumping In

Now you may ask, 'How can a small baby who can't yet sit up begin jumping-in exercises?' Well, let me explain that the principle of these exercises is to show how much confidence your baby has and that he shows no fear of going into the water. It is marvellous to see a young baby wriggling forward with a grin on his face and splashing into the pool towards mum and dad.

Small babies

Babies of under six months, unable to sit up, must be placed on the very edge of the pool with you in the water supporting them under their arms at all times. Now introduce a new game which your baby will begin to associate with jumping in, i.e. counting slowly, one . . . two . . . three . . . and lifting him up and into the water, then straight up and back on to the side. Do this two or three times to see how baby reacts. Now allow your baby to do the same exercise and this time put him right under and let him surface by himself as explained earlier under 'Submersion and release' on page 38. Well done! Remember: keep practising and have fun when you do this routine.

Six to ten months

9.1 First stage in learning to jump in. The mother reassures her baby and holds her all the time.

As soon as your baby is able to sit up on his own, place him on the edge of the pool comfortably. Now move a short distance

away from the pool edge yourself and call your baby — even clap your hands, because you may find that while he is sitting on the poolside his attention may wander, especially if he is a 'show-off' as many babies are. They seem to like to capture an audience before they jump in!

9.2 Mother guides baby into the water to introduce him to jumping in.

9.3 Second stage of jumping in with a toddler – no holding hands, but lots of encouragement.

As soon as baby has made up his mind, the slightest wriggle forward will be enough for him to fall into the pool. This can be a great game for most babies and they thrive on it. Some babies will still need coaxing, however, and if yours is one of these, try letting him hold on to just one of your fingers and you can assist until he feels happy to do the exercise unaided. Remember to allow baby to go right under and surface by himself.

9.4–5 Obviously water holds no fear for this little girl.

Walking baby

Some babies mature a lot earlier than others; therefore some babies of ten months are already walking and would now be able to stand and walk into the pool. They are still too young to make the actual movement of jumping in, but because they have no fear they will simply walk to the edge and throw themselves off! So beware that the pool area is clear of any other bathers and that it is safe for baby to 'walk in'. Again, encourage this confidence and allow baby to swim first before you pick him up.

Safety

Obviously some pools are perfect for these jumping-in exercises, but there are certain pools where *you must be careful.*

Deck-level pools (where the water level reaches the very top and in some cases overlaps) are ideal. Hazards are apparent, however, in the type of swimming pools that have the water level lower than the deck — sometimes a difference of about 50 centimetres/18 inches or more. The problem here is the drop that baby has to make before he reaches the water! Some pools also have a rail in the water which has to be missed clearly before baby is safe to jump alone. In these cases, until your baby is jumping forward and *well clear* of the edge, I would start him off on the swimming-pool steps, which are normally nearer the water's edge or, in some cases, actually in the water.

Remember: before you do these exercises, the safety of your baby is always the first priority.

9.6 'One . . . two . . . three!' Adam Hawley, aged eighteen months, prepares to jump in.

9.7 'Here I go . . .'
(Note depth of water.)

10 Swimming Aids

There are many swimming aids available today which encourage young children to learn to swim.

Armbands

These are by far the most popular aid. Unfortunately, many parents have no idea as to how they should be used, tending to allow their children, even tiny babies, to wear armbands all the time. This, of course, discourages their natural ability to float and therefore total dependence is put upon the aids whenever a child visits the swimming pool. Some children have been known to rely on armbands as a swimming aid for six or seven years and obviously, as a swimming teacher, I have found it very hard to convince that child to take them off.

Do remember, if you use armbands, to allow your small child to wear them for only short periods of time. 'Ten minutes on, ten minutes off' is an excellent guide, and soon your child will actually start to explore his own ability without them. Also, as your child becomes more confident, release some air from the armbands so that they are not always fully inflated: this, in turn, allows the child to lie closer to the water and not so high up. Less air often allows freer movement of the arms too.

Certainly armbands are a tremendous asset as a teaching aid, but care and consideration must be given as to how and when they are to be used.

10.1 Short sessions
with armbands and
toys can encourage
a reluctant swimmer.

10.2 Coaxing a young
swimmer with the aid
of armbands.

10.3 Floats can be used to help develop a kicking movement.

10.4 A supporting hand from mother helps baby to swim along with a float.

Rubber rings

There are many types of rings available, from the normal single-channel type to the large inflatable ones that resemble ducks, hippos and other such animals. These are great fun for toddlers and older children, but please take care when using them. Some children have been known to have the frightening experience of slipping quickly through the centre of a ring, leaving it above them. Certainly, if your child likes the ring, let him have one: but again, as with armbands, don't let him stay in one for too long. Short 'fun' sessions are the ideal approach with this kind of swimming aid.

Floats

Floats can be used successfully with very young children for encouraging a kicking movement, but because a child needs to grip a float, he should be at least one year old before using one.

New swim harness

The new swim harness (patent number 8314847) invented by the author of this book is designed for parents who wish to take very young babies and toddlers, aged three months to five years, to swimming pools. The harness enables the child to be carried around in the water quite safely while mum and dad have a swim. It gives the child tremendous confidence as it removes the fear of falling into the pool and enables him to feel the water around his body as the parent swims along. The harness is fully adjustable with a quick-release belt and baby can be carried on your front or on your back. It should come onto the market in the near future.

11 Future Aims

Your ultimate aim with a young baby must be to see him swimming unaided, quite happily and safely, in the swimming pool. By now you and your child will be used to the audience and the comments of admiration from friends and other members of the public. Above all, you know that you have given your baby a chance to survive, if he were to enter deep water accidentally and unsupervised. As described earlier, the under-fives are very much at risk where water is concerned, but together you have gained confidence in this element — and a lot of fun meanwhile. After all, I believe your baby could always swim: he simply needed the opportunity to show you how it's done! And when he's learned, you can continue your swim sessions together for as long as you like — certainly, health-wise both you and your baby will prosper.

11.1 'Shh . . . don't tel anyone, but I can swim

Appendices

Observation Chart

For use with submersion exercises)

Date of birth	Boy or girl		COMMENTS
EYES	Open	Closed	
MOUTH	Open	Closed	
BUBBLES	Nose	Mouth	
REACTION	Calm	Crying	
RECOVERY	Good	Poor	
PARENTS	Confident	Unsure	

General Progress Guide

Please remember that some babies take longer than others to learn to swim, so be patient. The guide below is only an outline.

Six to ten weeks	Swimming and submersion in the bath at home Floating, front and back position
Three months	2–5 metres/2–5½ yards and floating Swimming in a circle round your body
Four to six months	Deep swims: 5–8 metres/5½–9 yards Jumping in (early stages)
Six to ten months	8–10 metres/9–11 yards, with ease Jumping in (advanced stages) All other general exercises including floating and deep swims
One year to eighteen months	Longer distances, correct breathing (approximately 25 metres/27 yards) Swimming on back and front Jumping in
Eighteen months and over	Aim for 100 metres/108 yards and over

Swim Sessions - Recommended Duration

Three to six months

First visit: ten minutes only
Second/third visit: fifteen minutes only
Fourth/fifth visit: twenty minutes only
Sixth visit onwards: thirty minutes - no longer
Do not allow your baby to get cold

Six to nine months

First visit: fifteen minutes only
Second/third visit: fifteen to twenty minutes
Fourth/fifth visit: twenty to twenty-five minutes
Sixth visit onwards: thirty minutes

Nine months and over

First visit: fifteen minutes only
Second/third visit: twenty minutes only
Fourth/fifth visit: twenty-five minutes only
Sixth visit onwards: thirty minutes only

Thirty minutes is ample for young babies — after all, you don't want them to catch cold or become exhausted. And remember: always leave the pool when baby is happy and not if he is upset.

A confident Savlon
Water Baby about to
enjoy a dip?

Savlon Water Baby Award Scheme

The aim of the National Savlon Water Baby Scheme is to reduce infant drownings. The National Savlon Water Baby Awards, organised jointly by Savlon and the Amateur Swimming Association, are for all children up to the age of five. These awards are special badges for your baby's swimming costume. They can only be gained through recognised parent and baby classes held under the direction of an ASA approved teacher.

Award 1 A Savlon Water Baby Badge with turquoise blue design will be awarded to a baby who swims a width or 10 metres with swimming aids.

Award 2 A Savlon Water Baby Badge with dark blue design will be awarded to a baby who swims half a width or 5 metres without swimming aids.

Write to the Amateur Swimming Association (Savlon Water Baby Awards), Harold Fern House, Derby Square, Loughborough, Leicestershire LE11 0AL for further information.

**Savlon Water Babies
are safer babies**

Index